Keep It Real

Reality Based Self Defense, Philosophies, Principles and Applications

Author:
Kevin Batchelor

Keep It Real

Reality Based Self Defense, Philosophies, Principles and Applications

Author:
Kevin Batchelor

Principle Editors
Kevin Batchelor, Robin Batchelor, Lori Jacobwith

Graphic Designer: Kim Babbitt
Technique Photographer: Lily Batchelor
Demonstration Partner: Paul Worlitz

City of Publication
St. Charles, Missouri USA

1st Edition
ISBN-13: 979-8-218-29492-2
LCCN: 2023919116

Warning: The author and the publisher are in no way responsible for injuries including death or any misuse of the information found in this book. This book is for educational purposes only. Examples found in this book are at your own risk. Consult your physician before starting any new exercise program or physical activity.

Table of Contents

Dedication

This book is dedicated to my wife Robin and my daughter Lily.

Special Thanks

I want to thank God for giving me willpower and determination. I would like to thank my wife Robin and my daughter Lily for their support during all of my hours of training and writing. I want to thank Sifu Ken Sills, Professor Charlie Walton, Guro Allan Wiggins, Guro Erol Weber, Sensei Neil Sutton, and Sensei Michael Scott for sharing their knowledge. I would also like to thank Paul Worlitz for his time helping me with the photographs throughout this book.

Preface

Growing up in a small town in Southern Missouri during the 80's and early 90's, my first exposure to martial arts was through the movies. I remember, at way too young of an age, my mom and dad taking me to the theater to see a Chuck Norris double feature, Silent Rage, and Lone Wolf McQuade. From that point forward, I was hooked on martial arts movies. At this time, there were no martial arts schools in the area. Within a couple of years, a gentleman named William "Buddy" Colburn opened a Taekwondo school. I convinced my parents to sign me up for classes. I became very dedicated. After approximately two years of training in Taekwondo, I competed in several tournaments in Paducah, Kentucky and Dyersburg, Tennessee. Unfortunately, for personal reasons, Sensei Colburn closed his school. My martial arts training ceased. It was not until adulthood that my interest in fitness and martial arts training rekindled. I became heavily involved in Kajukenbo, followed by Jun Fan Gung Fu/Jeet Kune Do, Kali, Western Boxing, Shotokan Karate, and Cabales Serrada.

I initially became involved in endurance training and long-distance running, but I needed more. I began investigating various martial arts schools in the area. Ohana Martial Arts owned by Sifu Ken Sills was the first to intrigue me. I met with Sifu Ken on Monday before his evening class. It was an art I had never heard of called Kajukenbo. Interestingly enough, it was an American martial art formed in Hawaii between 1947 and 1949 composed of Karate, Judo, Jujitsu, Kenpo, Kung Fu, and Western Boxing. It turned out to be a high-energy, reality-based art that pushed the mind and the body. It was exactly what I was looking for in a martial art. I trained for 4 years under Sifu Ken. This unique blended style from

Hawaii gave me a solid foundation that allowed me to easily pick up other styles. After training Kajukenbo, I visited a school called Apex Martial Arts which had a strong Jeet Kune Do and Filipino Martial Arts influence. Right away I took to Guro Allan Wiggins. Guro Allan had been training in these arts for 20 years but his martial arts training dated back 50 years. Guro Allan was a wealth of knowledge. To this day, I regularly train in JKD, FMA, and Western Boxing under Guro Allan.

During the same period as my training with Guro Allan, I began training in Shotokan Karate under Sensei Neil Sutton and Sensei Michael Scott at the Community Karate Center located in St. Charles, Missouri. This gave me a new understanding of range and body dynamics.

Through Guro Allan, I met Guro Erol Weber, an instructor of Cabales Serrada, of which I am currently a student at the St. Louis Kali Academy.

The self-defense philosophies, principles, and applications found in this book are variations derived from the teachings of the instructors that I have had the privilege and pleasure to train under as well as independent study of my own. I hope you enjoy reading it as much as I enjoyed writing it.

How To Use the Book

Begin by reading and understanding the philosophies and principles discussed in Chapter 1, Chapter 2, and Chapter 3. Before starting the grab defenses, punch defenses and weapon defenses, you should become familiar with the open-hand techniques, the closed-hand techniques, and the leg techniques discussed in this book. If you do not have equipment, these techniques can be practiced in front of a mirror. Once you are comfortable with these techniques, you will need a partner to train the various defenses. You and your partner should not use real weapons during this training. Foam sticks and plastic training knives are readily available online for purchase.

Keep in mind, the scenarios in this book are prescribed scenarios. Acts of violence are dynamic. The purpose of the scenarios is to provide you with possibilities, and hopefully some level of comfort if you encounter such a situation. Start slowly with no resistance as you and your partner work through each defense scenario. This will allow you to build good form and muscle memory. Once you are flowing smoothly with no resistance, gradually have your partner increase resistance. If you never fail, your partner is not resisting enough, and you are not learning! If you can perform a defense with your partner providing 80% resistance and you fail 80% of the time, begin experimenting on failed attempts. Think of the weapons of your body and how you might use them to survive those failed attempts. This will teach you to be adaptable. Remember, training is the time to experiment. You are in a safe environment with a trusted training partner.

Chapter 1 – Introduction

What is self-defense? Self-defense is the act of protecting yourself from unprovoked harm. It is preserving your physical well-being. Self-defense is not a mutual agreement to fight. If you have the opportunity to walk away or avoid the conflict in any way, it is not self-defense. For example, if you are confronted and asked to step outside, and you accept, it becomes a consensual fight. You could have just said no and stayed inside until your confronter decided to leave or just forgot about you. If you decline and do not step outside, you have successfully defended yourself. You have avoided the conflict. If you are attacked or know an attack is imminent, then physically defending yourself is the only solution. In this situation, your goal is not to stand toe-to-toe with your attacker. Your goal is to defend yourself in such a way you can buy time to escape. Self-defense is **NOT** a sport. It is **NOT** a chance to show you are a better fighter than your attacker. You may or may not be a better fighter. You may be smaller, weaker, or outnumbered, but your goal is to distract, injure, or both so that you can escape safely.

Key Points

- Self-defense is not a consensual fight.
- Self-defense is not meant for you to stand toe-to-toe fighting your attacker.
- Self-defense is meant to buy time to escape.
- Self-defense is protecting yourself.
- Self-defense situations can occur quickly.
- Self-defense situations are brutal.
- Self-defense is necessary when the attack is imminent.

Who can defend themself? You do not have to be a martial artist to defend yourself. Many traditional martial artists do not train to the level required for self-defense. They train fighting concepts for sport but often leave out reality-based self-defense concepts and key elements surrounding the psychology of self-defense. We also live in a softer world than the founders of these arts. People, specifically in the west, are not living in constant fear of war and defending themselves. There are no more samurai. Most people are not willing to train at extremely high levels. People do not want to go into the office with bruises and black eyes. Therefore, many martial artists today train primarily for art and light contact sports. An argument might be made that mixed martial arts (MMA) is a valid form of self-defense, but from a self-defense standpoint, MMA is not self-defense training either. There are several key reasons MMA is not self-defense training. MMA is training for sport. Every MMA fighter is training for a situation that they expect to live through. MMA has rules. There are no rules on the street. MMA fighters typically train a significant amount of grappling. On the street, with the potential of multiple attackers, grappling could get you seriously injured. Everyone should have some level of grappling knowledge, but it may not be the best option with multiple attackers and hard pavement. MMA is trained under high pressure which is great for self-defense, but MMA does not train a key element of self-defense and that is escaping. MMA trains to win the fight. MMA does not train to escape. With this training approach, you will not likely escape at your first opportunity. MMA does not train to defend against weapons either. On the street, you could encounter a weapon. Also, in a self-defense situation, you should always draw attention to yourself. You must let anyone within screaming distance know you need help. MMA fighters have no reason to scream for help. They train for sport. Karate on the other hand has its kia. A Karateka would be more likely to scream during a self-defense situation than an MMA fighter. Essentially, what you do in training, you will do under pressure. If you train ground fighting heavily, ground fighting will be a go-to for you. If you do not train to escape, you will not escape at your first chance. If you do not train to draw attention to yourself, you will not scream when you are attacked.

So how can you defend yourself if you are not a martial artist? This will hopefully become clear as you delve into this book.

Chapter 2 – Self Defense Concepts

- Verbal De-escalation
- Situational Awareness
- Evasion
- Flight
- Fight

Verbal De-escalation

Verbal de-escalation is the act of trying to verbally calm the situation. If you decide to use verbal de-escalation, ensure the range from your aggressor is such that he or she cannot physically reach you. I recommend right outside of kicking range. You should pay close attention during this time, and manage your distance. (**Note:** Range will be discussed in more detail later.) Do not let your aggressor encroach on your personal space. During this time your hands should be raised with your palms facing inward toward your face as if you are pleading with your aggressor. This hand position does not appear threatening to your aggressor or anyone looking from the outside. However, keeping your hands up provides you with protection from a possible attack. From the hands-up position, you can more readily deflect a strike or strike your aggressor if needed. Keeping your palms turned toward your face also protects vital arteries. If your aggressor happens to have a bladed weapon and your hands are facing palms out, you have major arteries exposed. Keeping your palms facing in will only expose the back side of your hands and arms which are mostly skin and bone. You may get cut but nothing vital will be damaged.

Situational Awareness

Situational awareness is one of the key elements of self-defense. Situational awareness is a simple concept. It means being aware of your surroundings. Be aware of the people around you. Be aware of vehicles near you. Be aware of the neighborhoods that you enter. It sounds simple, but with the distractions of today's world such as smartphones, tablets, and social media, it can become all too easy to become distracted and miss signs of danger. Criminals target people who look like victims. A criminal is more likely to target an individual standing on a street corner or sitting in a car focusing on their phone than someone who is alert. Criminals target low-hanging fruit. They are in search of easy prey.

Tips

1. Avoid distractions.
    a. Phones
    b. Tablets
    c. Laptops
2. Be vigilant.
    a. Parking lots
    b. ATMs
    c. Suspicious vehicles
    d. Suspicious people
3. Look for well-lit areas.
4. Stick to crowds.

Evasion

Evasion is a tactic that works hand in hand with situational awareness. This is different from escaping a direct attack or an imminent attack. Evasion is a proactive tactic. Waiting for an attack and then attempting to flee would be a reactive tactic. Evasion requires you to be aware of your surroundings and make sound judgment calls. Pay attention to the people and vehicles around you. For example, don't walk between vehicles in a parking lot. You should stick to the main isles. You are partially hidden from view as you walk between vehicles and it is much easier to be abducted or assaulted. Pay attention to the neighborhoods that you enter. The moment you feel uncomfortable, change your path proactively before you encounter danger. Never put yourself in a situation where you have to be reactive.

Tips

1. Be proactive.
    a. Avoid high-crime areas.
    b. Avoid suspicious people or vehicles.
    c. Follow your instincts. If it does not feel safe, change your path.

Flight

Unlike evasion, flight is a reactive tactic. Flight is attempting to escape from a dangerous situation. Flight is a tactic that is used if your evasion skills fail. In a best-case scenario, you are capable of running and escaping. However, this is not always the case. Suppose you are on a staircase, in a dead-end alley, against a wall or you have your family with you and you cannot run. In this situation, you cannot take flight and run without injuring your aggressor. In self-defense, flight should **ALWAYS** directly follow fight. You do not fight to show you are a better fighter. You fight to escape. You may have to injure your attacker to escape. An attacker may be able to fight through pain but a true injury should stop your attacker long enough to escape.

Fight

What dictates it is time to fight? The number one indicator is that you have already been assaulted. You have been pushed, punched, kicked, grabbed, etc. The realization that an attack is imminent is another indicator. Signs of an imminent attack are aggressive body language, yelling, and/or encroaching on one's personal space. These are signs that it may be time to act. Keep in mind attacking someone who has not yet physically assaulted you may have legal implications, but it may be the best choice to keep you and the people around you safe. The decision to fight is a judgment call that you will have to make under pressure.

The subject of fighting and the philosophies and principles surrounding it will be covered in more detail in Chapter 3 – Fighting Concepts.

Chapter 3 – Fighting Concepts

- Range
- Footwork
- 12 Weapons of the Body
- Centerline Theory
- Pain Principle
- High-Low Principle
- Properties of Surviving Violence

Range

There are 5 ranges of attack. You should be aware of these ranges, and at all times know your range. This will allow you to know what your attacker is capable of doing to you and what you are capable of doing to your attacker.

1. Weapon range – This range encompasses anything from a baseball bat to a gun. From this range, you can be assaulted with any long-range weapon. You can also counter your attacker using any long-range weapon.
2. Kicking range - This range is slightly closer than the weapon range. From this range, your attacker cannot easily punch you without closing the distance. However, your attacker can make contact with a kick. You can reach your attacker with a kick as well. To use your hands, you will have to close the distance between you and your attacker.
3. Punching range - This range begins to get closer. Now your attacker can punch you or you can punch your attacker.
4. Elbow/Trapping range - From this range, you or your attacker can now strike with elbows or trap and control one another.
5. Grappling range - This is the closest range. From this range, you can grab or be grabbed and taken to the ground.

Footwork

The fighter with the best footwork will dominate the fight. If you can outmaneuver your attacker, you have an advantage. If you have a good stance, you have better balance and are better situated to move and generate power. Good footwork also creates unpredictable movement. Good footwork also allows you to set up range, position, and angle. Good range, position, and angle give you a significant advantage over your opponent. If you control the range, you control the fight.

Boxing Fighting Stance

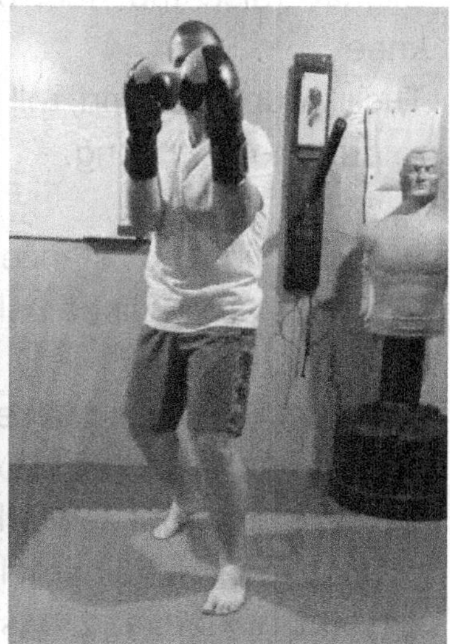

1. Bring your hands up with the elbows in tight to the body.
2. Blade your body. **Note:** Blading the body gives your opponent a smaller striking surface than standing square.

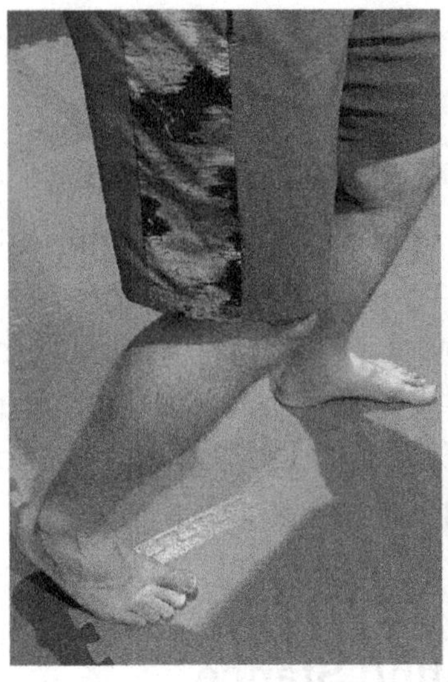 

3. Slightly raise the heel of your rear foot and bend your knees.
4. Tuck your chin and roll your shoulders forward. This is referred to as turtling.

Once in your fighting stance, begin to move around. The movement rules are outlined below.

1. Keep your body as relaxed as possible. Relaxation equals speed, and tension will exhaust you quickly.
2. Never cross your feet when stepping. Crossing your feet will put you in a vulnerable position.
3. Assuming a left lead, basic footwork is as follows:
    a. Moving left, step with the left foot first. This is your lead foot when in a left lead.
    b. Moving right, step with your right foot first. This is your rear foot when in a left lead.
    c. When moving forward, drive off your rear leg, stepping with your lead foot first.

d. When moving backward, drive off your front leg, stepping with your rear foot backward.
e. Always remember, as counterintuitive as it may initially seem, that your rear leg controls the distance from your opponent.
f. Take small steps. When moving left or right, limit the size of your step to the width of your foot. When moving forward or backward, limit the size of your step to half the length of your foot.
g. Always keep a consistent distance between your feet in your stance.

Shotokan Karate Fighting Stance

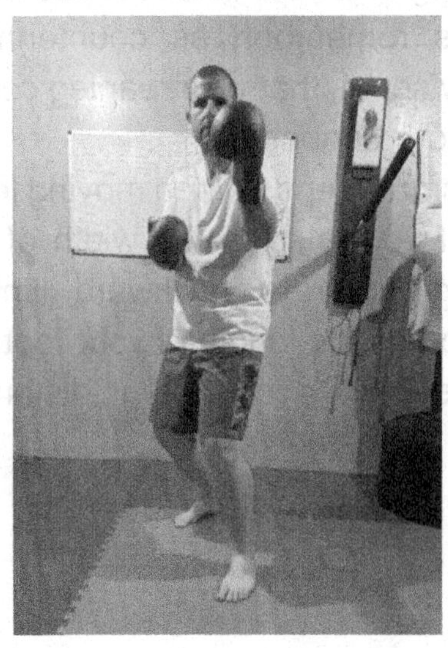

In this book, I primarily focus on the boxing fighting stance. However, due to my Shotokan Karate training, I also want to explain the Shotokan fighting stance.

1. The Shotokan Karate stance is similar to the boxing stance; however, the stance is deeper and slightly wider. My Shotokan Karate stance is not quite as low as others you may see.
2. The stance provides a connection to the ground for stability and the generation of power. The rear leg or lead leg, depending on the direction you are moving, should be running like an engine waiting for the brake to be released for explosive movement.
3. The lead hand is held up and out away from the body. This is your main blocking hand. The idea is to catch the strike early and as far from your body as possible.

4. The rear hand is back but lower than a boxer's rear hand. It gives direction like the barrel of a gun. This is the power hand and is chambered and ready to fire.
5. The head is stacked directly over the body. The chin is not tucked and the shoulders are not turtled. Shotokan fighters tend to manage distance, staying out of the inside as much as possible, and using explosive in and out attacks. Their goal, if possible, is a one-strike finishing blow to their attacker.

12 Weapons of the Body

Most people become preoccupied with their hands and feet, but in reality, you have 12 weapons that can be used. You should use any weapon available to injure your attacker. Starting at the head and working down the body, I have listed all 12 weapons.

1. Head (strike/control)
2. Mouth (bite)
3. Chin (control)
4. Shoulders (control/strike)
5. Elbows (control/strike)
6. Forearms (strike/control/blocking)
7. Hands (strike/control/blocking)
8. Hips (control)
9. Butt (control)
10. Knees (strike/control)
11. Shins (strike/blocking)
12. Feet (strike/control/blocking)

In addition to the 12 weapons of the body, I will add another weapon that is readily available to every person. This weapon is the force of gravity and the earth. If you are in a situation where you can or must take your opponent to the ground, you must provide a downward driving force that adds to the natural force of gravity. Remember, force equals mass times acceleration. This combined force will make your attacker feel as if the earth itself is his enemy and has just delivered a devastating blow.

Centerline Theory

Centerline theory is a key element of Wing Chun Kung Fu and Filipino Martial Arts. The centerline is an imaginary vertical line that divides the body into two halves. Centerline theory is vital offensively and defensively. Offensively, many important targets are on the centerline such as eyes, nose, chin, throat, sternum, stomach, and groin. These targets are key in self-defense. In addition to these targets, although not directly on the center line, knees are a vital target. The centerline also plays a role in maximizing striking power. When your centerline is positioned on your target, you will generate more power. Defensively, blocks are more effective when your centerline is positioned on your attacker's strike. You should strive to control your opponent's centerline while keeping your centerline on your target at all times.

Pain Principle

The pain principle is a simple concept. Every strike is meant to inflict pain and every block is meant to inflict pain. If your attacker throws a punch and you block with enough power to cause pain, he or she will think twice about throwing the same technique again.

High-Low Principle

The high-low principle is a confusion technique. Vary the level of your attack to keep your opponent guessing. For example, a high jab followed by a low kick, or a cross followed by a hook to the ribs, and then return with an uppercut to the chin. The idea is to remove the predictability of your movements.

Properties of Surviving Violence

The properties of surviving a violent encounter can be broken into two categories, mental and physical. Each category has different elements. If an element is removed, the survival rate drops. You can think of mental and physical as being at two opposite ends of a spectrum. The person with the best chance of survival is the person who has mental strength, as well as being capable technically and physically. As the mental side and the physical side come closer together, the survival rate increases. You may be a physically strong, technically proficient fighter but if you are mentally weak due to fear, stress, anxiety, or panic during a life-or-death situation, you will likely fail to successfully defend yourself. The opposite is true as well. You may be mentally strong with nerves of steel but have no fighting ability. Rather than mental strength, you will likely fail due to your lack of training, unless you and your attacker are at the same physical and technical level. If you are both at the same physical and technical level and you are mentally strong, you will likely fare better than the trained fighter who is mentally weak.

1. Mental
    a. You must have mental strength. You must be able to look beyond your fear, stress, and anxiety to complete the task in front of you.
    b. You must believe you will survive the encounter. Self-doubt is not an option.
    c. Be aware of your surroundings.
        i. Exit routes
        ii. Obstacles between you and escape
        iii. Number of attackers
        iv. Potential weapons

   d. Think strategically. Although things happen quickly, use your knowledge of your surroundings and your knowledge of self-defense to develop your strategy. Keep your strategy simple, remember this is under pressure and violent attacks are dynamic. Your strategy may have to change so be resilient.

2. Physical
   a. Attack with full power.
   b. Manage your distance.
   c. Do not create patterns. Use unpredictable movement.
   d. Your responses must be trained so they are second nature.

Chapter 4 – Basic Open Hand Striking

- Palm Strike
- Tiger Claw
- Palm-Down Chop
- Palm-Up Chop
- Forearm Strike (Brachial Stun)
- Horizontal Elbow Strike
- Vertical Elbow Strike

Palm Strike

1. Start in a fighting stance.
2. Tighten your right hand by bending the fingers at the 2nd joint, squeeze your fingers together, and tilt your wrist back approximately 75 degrees.
3. With full momentum and full rotation, strike in an upward motion beneath the chin with the palm of your hand.
4. The palm strike can also target the nose or the jawline.

Tiger Claw

1. Steps 1 through 3 are identical to the palm strike.
2. Once the strike is fully extended, with a rigid hand, rake your fingertips down the eyes and face.

Palm-Down Chop

1. Start in a fighting stance.
2. With the non-striking hand up guarding the face, point your elbow at your target. Your elbow should be treated like the sight of a gun and your hand is the bullet.

3. Create a rigid open hand by tensing and squeezing your fingers tightly together.
4. Extend your arm outward toward your target. In this case, strike the side of the neck targeting the carotid artery. If hit hard enough, you can cause a disruption of blood flow potentially leading to a knockout.
5. This strike is not powered by the arms alone but the power should be generated from the rear leg up through the body. Body rotation is critical for power.

Palm-Up Chop

1. When learning the palm-up chop, begin by placing your striking hand with the palm facing up at your ear as shown in the picture above. Your other hand should be protecting your face. Once muscle memory is developed, you do not have to start at the ear. You can and will shorten the motion.
2. Driving off your rear leg, rotate your body and arm toward your target striking with the edge of your hand, not your fingers. Your hand should be tight and rigid on impact. The throat and the carotid arteries are excellent targets for this strike.
3. A palm-up chop to the throat could potentially collapse the windpipe. Without an emergency tracheotomy, a collapsed windpipe will cause death. If you are not in a life-or-death situation, the carotid artery on either side of the neck is a better target.

Forearm Strike (Brachial Stun)

1. This technique is similar to the palm-down chop.
2. From a fighting stance, point your elbow toward the target, in this case, the neck.
3. The other hand should be raised protecting your face.
4. With a closed fist, driving off your rear foot, rotate your body and extend your arm striking the brachial plexus. The brachial plexus is a group of nerves that supply function to the shoulder, arm, and hand.

Horizontal Elbow Strike

1. From a left lead, drive off the rear leg, rotating your body as your right elbow raises to a horizontal position.
2. Your right elbow should strike the left side of your opponent's face. **Note:** The left hand should be raised for protection. See the images for reference.

Vertical Elbow Strike

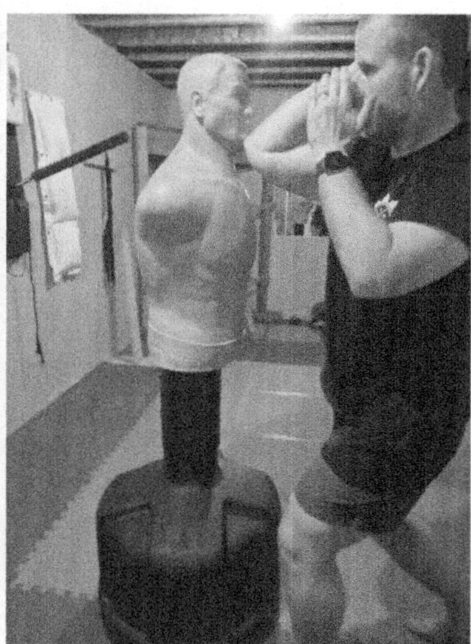

1. From a left lead, drive off the rear leg, rotating your body.
2. As your body rotates, raise your elbow vertically striking your opponent's chin. **Note:** Your elbow should follow the path of your centerline and your opponent's centerline. Power is generated by the rotation and the upward motion that is created by driving off the rear leg.

Chapter 5 – Basic Closed Hand Striking

- Boxing Jab/Cross Punch
- Karate Jab/Reverse Punch
- Vertical Punch

Making a Proper Fist

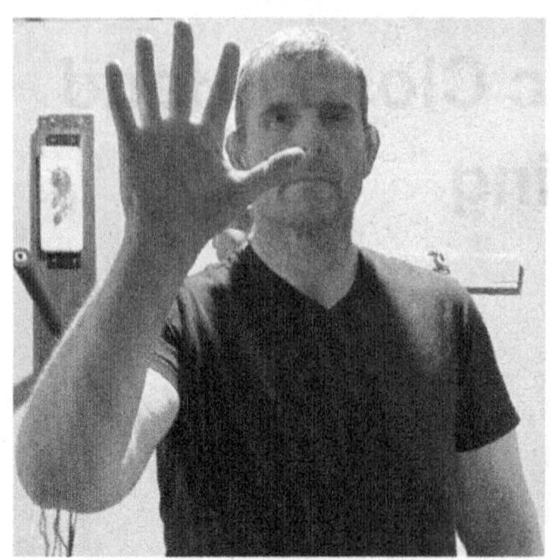

1. From an open hand, close your fist tightly. As shown in the picture above, wrap your thumb around the outside of the index finger and middle finger.
2. Never tuck your thumb on the inside of the fist. This can injure your thumb.
3. Never leave your thumb sticking out as if you are giving a thumbs up. This has the potential of catching on your target and severely injuring the thumb.

Proper Wrist Alignment Straight Punch

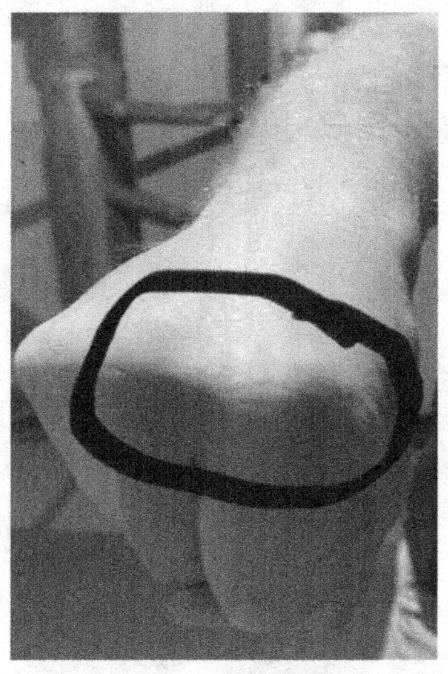

1. For a straight punch such as a jab or a cross, your wrist should be aligned in such a way that the thumb side of your fist is flush with the inside of your arm.
2. The top of your hand should be flush with the top of your arm.
3. As circled in the picture above, your alignment should support striking with the two largest knuckles.

Jab/Cross Straight Punch

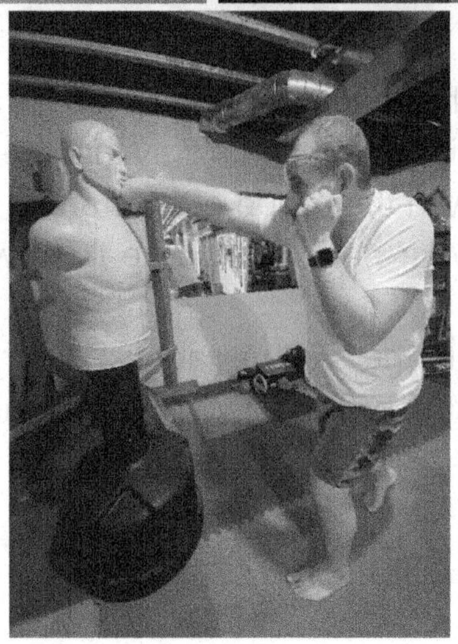

1. From a proper fighting stance, left or right lead.
    a. Tuck your chin.
    b. Bring your guard up.
        i. The lead hand should be slightly in front of you.

ii. The rear hand should be within a thumb's reach of your cheek.

2. Blade your body.
3. Your jab should drive from the ground up, engaging the hip of your lead side. You should have a slight pivot of the lead foot after the jab.
4. During your jab your rear hand should continue to protect your face. Do not drop your guard!
5. Your jab should snap out and immediately return to its starting position.
6. Your shoulder should roll up on your jab. This will provide extra reach but most importantly, cover for your jawline. See the images for reference.
7. Your cross should drive from the ground up utilizing pressure from your rear leg.
8. Your rear foot will have a slight pivot.
9. You should get maximum rotation of your torso.
10. Your shoulder should roll up on your cross. This will provide extra reach but most importantly, cover your jawline. See the images for reference.
11. During your cross your lead hand should continue to protect your face. Do not drop your guard!
12. Your cross should snap out and immediately return to its starting position.

Karate Style Jab/Reverse Punch

1. Similar to boxing, Karate also generates power from the ground up.
2. Karate uses the dynamic of hip rotation and/or momentum moving forward for the jab.
3. Karate does not roll the shoulder toward the jawline. It drops the shoulder and rolls the elbow downward to engage the latissimus muscles for maximum power generation.
4. Demonstrated in the above image, you see my non-striking hand on my hip. In a real engagement, the hand position would be raised but not as high as a boxer's guard.
5. The hand on the hip serves a purpose. It trains the Karateka to obtain maximum hip rotation when striking. It also trains the pulling hand. Suppose you have made a connection with your opponent's arm; this hand can act as the pull hand. Upon connection to the arm, you can grab the arm sliding your hand to the wrist. Then, pull the arm to your hip as you simultaneously strike.

6. Similar to boxing's cross is the Karate reverse punch.
7. For the reverse punch, Karate generates power from the ground up. Like boxing, the reverse punch uses the body dynamic of rotation but the shoulder stays down and does not roll towards the jawline. Again, this is to engage the latissimus muscle to create a body connection generating power.
8. Karate also uses a dynamic known as vibration for the reverse punch. This dynamic is more complicated and will not be covered at this level. If at some point you decide Karate is your path, you will be exposed to this dynamic in your dojo.

Proper Wrist Alignment Vertical Punch

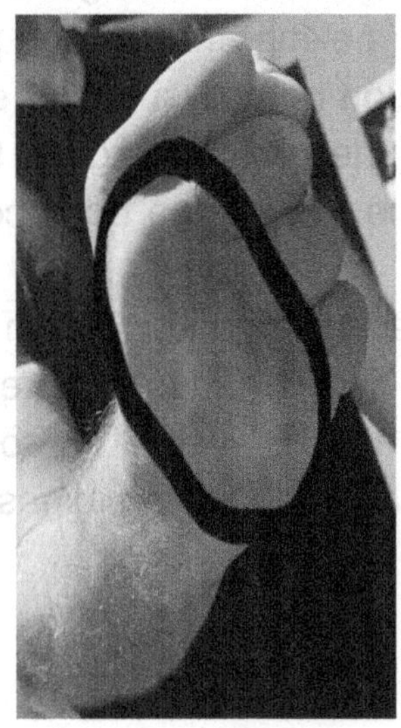

1. For a vertical punch, I prefer the Wing Chun alignment over the Kajukenbo and Karate alignment. Kajukenbo and Karate align the wrist to strike with the top two knuckles. Wing Chun aligns the wrist to strike with the bottom three knuckles. I feel the Wing Chin approach has a more natural feel.
2. Your fist should be aligned so the bottom edge of your hand is flush with the bottom of your arm. See the image for reference.
3. As circled in the picture above, your alignment should support striking with the three bottom knuckles.

Vertical Punch

1. I prefer the vertical punch for close range, closed hand striking to the face.
2. Like boxing and Karate, the power from this punch is generated from the ground up. It is like a pulse of energy traveling from the ground, through the leg and hip finishing on impact with the bottom three knuckles penetrating your target.
3. Your vertical punch should follow your centerline. This engages all necessary muscles and produces maximum striking power. Refer to the section on centerline theory.

Chapter 6 – Basic Leg Techniques

- Slant Kick
- Knee Stomp
- Knee Strike

Slant Kick

1. A slant kick, also known as an oblique kick, is typically used as a distraction drawing your attacker's attention down so you can attack high.
2. The kick is performed off the rear leg.
3. You should impact your attacker's shin with the inside of your foot.
4. This kick, although typically a distraction, can be painful if used as a shin scrape.
5. On contact, slide the inside of your shoe forcefully down your attacker's shin.

Knee Stomp

1. Similar to the slant kick, the knee stomp is performed off the rear leg.
2. This kick follows a similar motion as the slant kick but is intended to stomp and destroy the knee.

Knee Strike

1. Starting from a proper fighting stance, reach your lead hand along the side of your attacker's neck. Grasp the back of the neck. During this time, your other hand should be protecting your face. See the above images for reference.

2. Next, with your rear hand, reach along the other side of your attacker's neck grasping the back of the neck. Do not interlace your fingers. Place one hand over the other.
3. As shown in the third picture, securely clinch the neck. It is key you pull your elbows together as tightly as possible.
4. Simultaneously, pull your attacker downward as you strike with the knee.

Chapter 7 – Grab Attacks

Being grabbed is often the first contact made during an attack. Grabs are typically initiated by a larger, stronger attacker on a smaller, weaker victim. A small person typically does not grab a larger person. If you are grabbed, it is for control. Your attacker may use a grab to pull you along, or to hold you in place to strike. Your attacker may also grab you to throw you to the ground.

When attacked, men tend to be grabbed differently than women. A man will be grabbed for control to be punched, or to be thrown to the ground. Men typically don't grab other men by the wrist as a control tactic. Wrist grabs are typically performed on women by men.

A grab defense typically has 3 properties.

1. Strike
2. Re-grab
3. Finish

Upon being grabbed, you should immediately strike your attacker. You should target one of the vital areas mentioned in the section on centerline theory (eyes, nose, throat, groin, or knees). Your attack must be aggressive. It must be intended to injure your attacker. Use full mass and full body rotation. At this point, if you are released, you should immediately escape.

After striking your attacker, if unable to escape, you should immediately re-grab. The re-grab serves two purposes. The re-grab allows you to attain some level of control while at the same time psychologically taunting your attacker. Now your attacker is no longer in control. You have decided to strike and attach yourself directly to your aggressor. Now the finish property comes into play. This consists of consecutive strikes. At this point, you should follow what is called the high-low principle. If your first strike went to the throat, go low with the next strike attacking the knees or the groin. Then return high for the following strike and so on. The finish property can also consist of eye gouges, takedowns, locks, and breaks. Potentially you are fighting for your life, therefore anything to allow a successful escape is valid.

Below is a list of common grab attacks.

1. Single-hand collar grab
2. Cross-line wrist grab
3. Two-hand choke or collar grab
4. Two-hand choke against the wall
5. Inline wrist grab
6. Headlock
7. Bear hug - arms free
8. Bear hug - arms trapped

Single-Hand Collar Grab Defense 1

1. From a neutral position, Paul reaches to grab my right collar.
2. I step to his inside placing my center on his attacking arm and intercept his arm with my right hand. See the images for reference. This is not a hard stop but a slap. This slap is meant to deflect the grab to my collar. Keep in mind this same technique can work for any inline motion. A straight punch, such as a jab, is a good example.

3. As the slap deflects Paul's attacking arm, my hand bounces off performing a palm-down chop to the carotid artery. Think of the slap as a deflection that bounces like a trampoline, propelling the palm-down chop. This is called spring energy. Spring energy will increase speed and power.

Single-Hand Collar Grab Defense 2

1. This defense is very similar to the "Single-Hand Collar Grab Defense 1".
2. From a neutral position, Paul steps in to grab my right collar.
3. I step to his outside placing my center on his attacking arm intercepting his grab with my left hand. See the images for reference. This is not a hard stop but a slap. This slap is meant to deflect the grab to my collar. Keep in mind this same technique can work for any inline motion. A straight punch, such as a jab, is a good example.

4. As the slap deflects Paul's attacking arm, my hand bounces off performing a palm-down chop to the throat. Think of the slap as a deflection that bounces like a trampoline, propelling the palm-down chop. As mentioned in "Single Hand Collar Grab Defense 1", this is called spring energy and will increase speed and power.

Single-Hand Collar Grab Defense 3

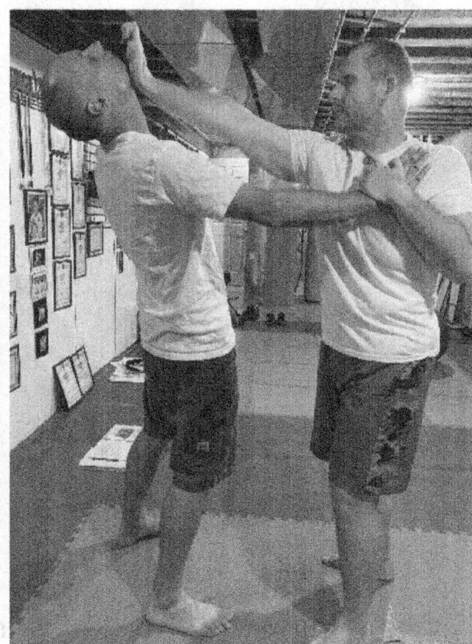

1. Paul reaches and grabs my left shoulder, attempting to control my movement to punch with a right straight.
2. I immediately re-grab Paul's hand, securing it to my body, and simultaneously perform a palm strike to his chin.
    a. The re-grab is as much a defensive tactic as it is a psychological tactic. The re-grab aids in removing the illusion of total control from the attacker.
    b. Although difficult to see, the re-grab securely grasps Paul's thumb pad. This is crucial to the next series of steps.

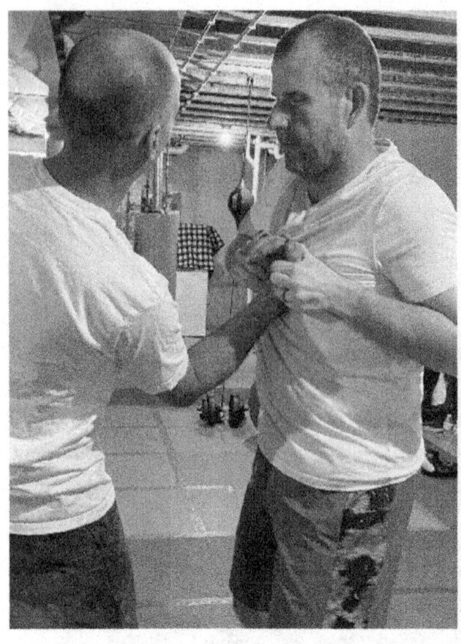

3. With Paul's thumb pad secured by my left hand during the re-grab, I roll Paul's left hand over keeping it tight to my body.
4. I now grab his left hand securely with my right hand.
5. My right hand should be placed so that my thumb is on the back side of his hand directly below the knuckles.
6. His hand must stay tight to my body.
7. I form a goose neck shape with his hand and wrist.
8. My body now turns in a corkscrew motion toward the ground. It is key that your momentum is driving toward the ground.

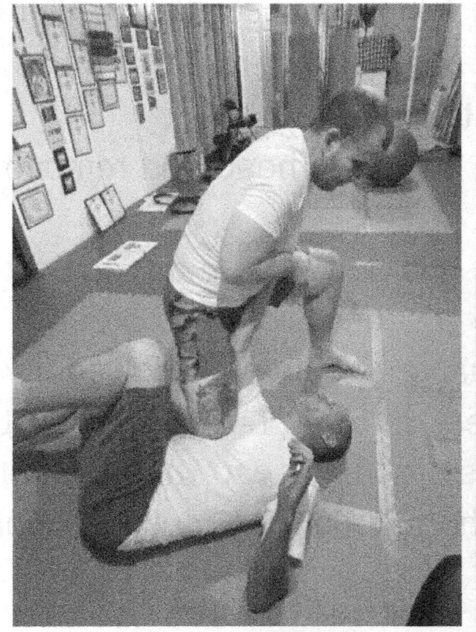

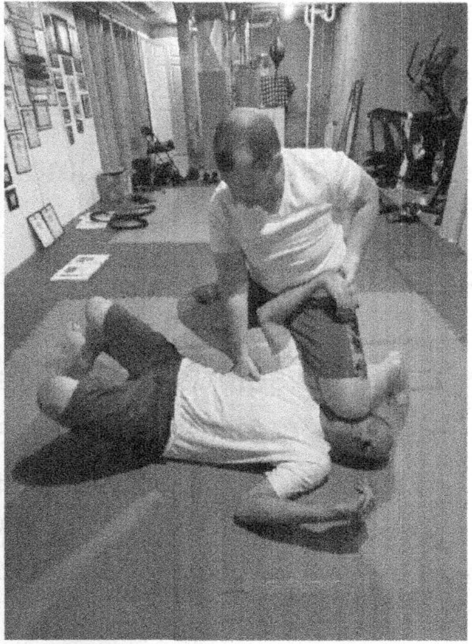

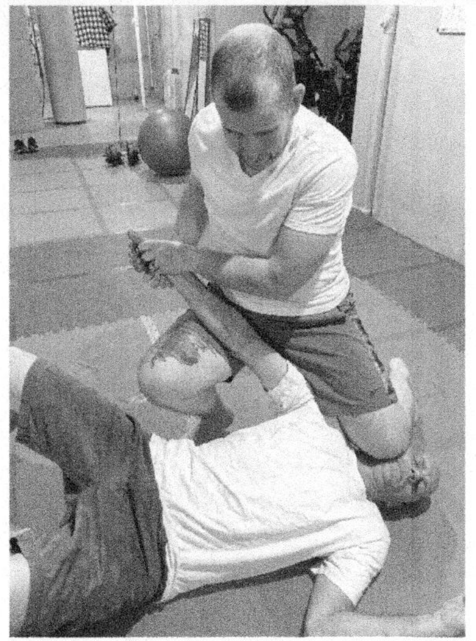

9. The corkscrew motion in conjunction with the downward pressure will take your attacker to the ground. If done with enough speed and force, it should break his or her wrist.
10. Once your attacker is on the ground, you must maintain control.

11. My knee is on his ribs applying pressure as I continue to control his arm. My other leg is away from his unsecured arm to prevent a potential takedown.
12. Next, I place my left knee on Paul's head and remove my right knee from his ribs.
13. I follow with a strike to the ribs and an arm bar against my right thigh. This could be a submission or a break. This being a self-defense situation, a break followed by an escape is likely your best choice, but use your best judgment. A submission is probably best when controlling a rowdy friend or uncle who has had too much to drink at the family barbeque.

Cross-Line Wrist Grab Defense

1. Paul reaches across my body performing a cross-line wrist grab to my right wrist.
2. I raise my left hand to guard my face.
3. Paul attempts to pull me forward.
4. I perform a slant kick or stomp to Paul's knee. This blow to the knee will collapse Paul forward.

5. After stomping the knee, I step behind Paul's leg performing a diagonal elbow strike to the side of his face while controlling his right arm.

6. With his right arm controlled and firmly attached to my hip, I perform a downward elbow strike to his spine.

7. Once Paul is no longer a threat, it is time to escape.

Two-Hand Choke/Collar Grab Defense 1

1. Paul attempts to execute a two-hand collar grab or a two-hand choke.
2. I intercept the grab or choke by bringing both of my arms through his and my centerline.
3. I spread my arms in an outward motion putting myself on his inside. This clears a path for the next technique. See the images for reference.

4. I perform a front kick to drive Paul back and create distance between the two of us.
   a. To execute the front thrust kick, raise your knee toward your chest maintaining a good posture. Try not to lean backward. The height of the knee will directly correlate with the height of the kick. The direction of the knee should be aimed at the target. Think of your knee as the sight of a gun and the distance from your hip to your knee as the barrel of the gun. The bullet is your foot. As you extend the kick, the power does not only come from the extension of the leg but comes from the ground up as you thrust your hips forward.

Tip: Try this technique with a two-hand shove attack to the chest.

Two-Hand Choke/Collar Grab Defense 2

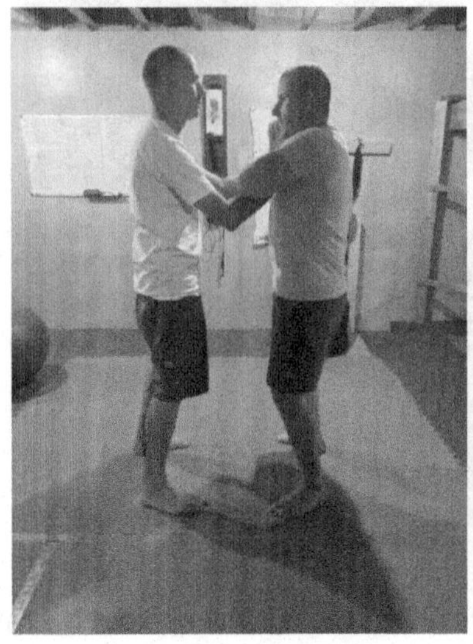

1. Paul attacks with a two-hand choke or collar grab.
2. With my left hand, I reach over the top of his arms securing both of his hands tightly to my body.

3. I then rotate my body to the left 90 degrees dropping my weight with a downward elbow strike across both of his arms.
4. With full body rotation, I take a step in with my right foot executing a right elbow strike to the side of Paul's head.

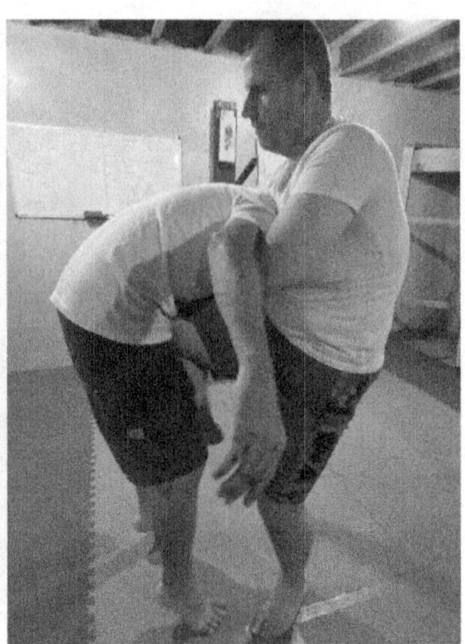

5. At this point, I wrap his neck with my right arm and knee him to the sternum.

6. Once Paul is no longer a threat, I escape.

Two-Hand Choke Against Wall Grab Defense

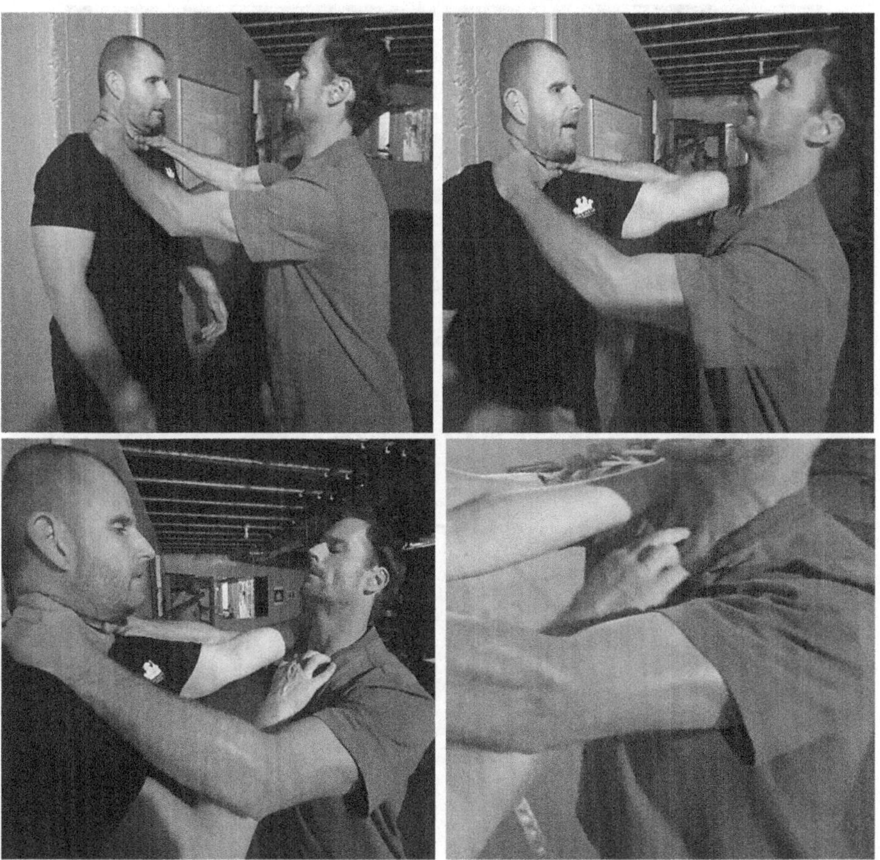

1. While securing the back of Paul's neck, I place my index or index and middle finger in the jugular nodule. See the image for reference.
2. I control the back of the neck pulling it forward and simultaneously driving the fingers inward and downward into the jugular nodule.

Inline Wrist Grab

1. Paul confronts me in a threatening manner.
2. I raise my hands with my palms positioned toward my face as if I am pleading.
3. Paul reaches and performs an inline wrist grab.

4. I drop my hand to my hip immediately, re-grabbing and raising his arm.

5. Upon the re-grab, I pull his arm and perform a vertical punch to his jawline. **Note:** A strike can proceed the re-grab.

Headlock Grab Defense

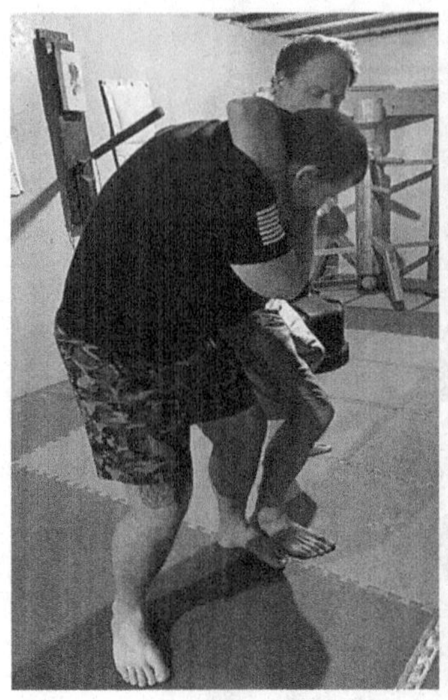

1. Paul puts me in a side headlock with his right arm.
2. I cover my face for protection with my right hand and reach around Paul's back with my left arm securing his striking arm with my left hand. See the above image for reference. **Note:** You can secure the striking arm from the inside of the attacker's arm if he or she is too large to secure from the outside.

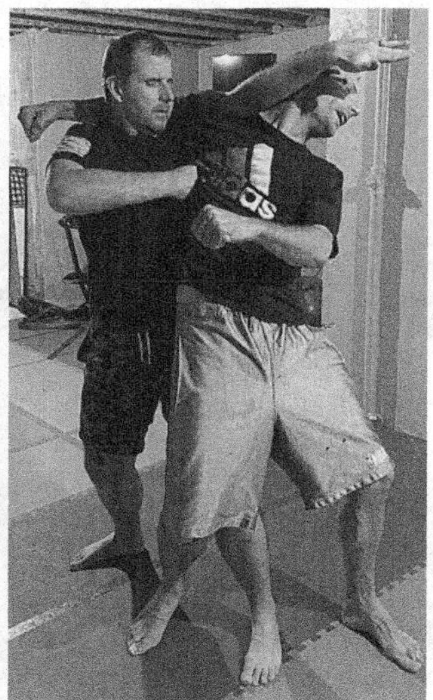

3. Once Paul's striking arm is secured, I pull it forcefully across his body in my direction. Simultaneously, with the pull of Paul's arm, I step my left foot behind his right foot. At the same time, perform a palm strike through his jawline. The palm strike should be in a downward trajectory. This will break his center backward.
4. My arm is the only thing supporting him.
5. I perform a punch to his rib cage.

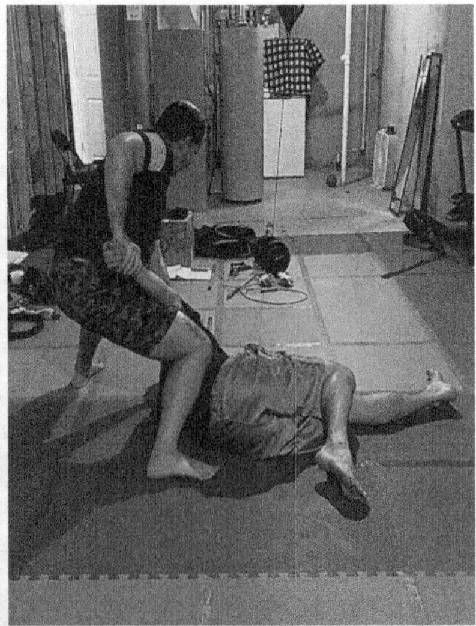

6. I reach back, securing Paul's right wrist with my right hand.
7. My left hand is currently facing with the palm toward Paul's face.
8. Simultaneously, I rotate my left hand so that the back of my hand turns in and downward into his face while rotating my left leg backward as if it were a gate and my right leg was a fence post.

9. With his center already broken backward and this downward pressure and rotation, Paul is taken to the ground.
10. From this point, I control his right arm across my thigh in an arm bar, while I strike to the face.

Bear Hug - Arms Free

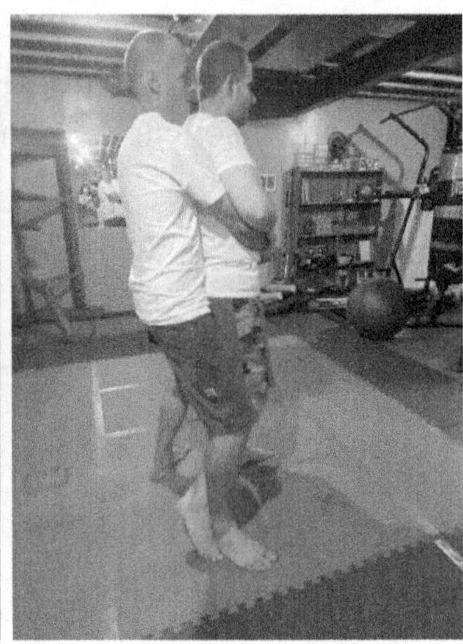

1. Paul grabs me in a bear hug with my arms free.
2. I immediately wrap my leg around the inside of his leg and push down on both of his wrists. This anchors me to Paul preventing a throw.

3. Anchored to Paul, I wait until I sense his body dropping from exhaustion.
4. I shoot my legs and hips out maintaining control of his wrists.

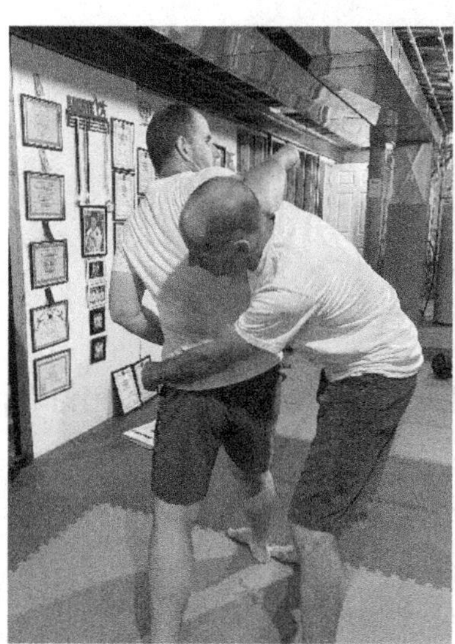
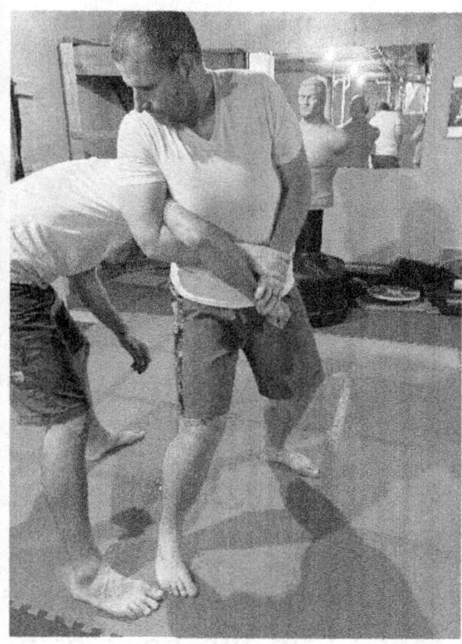

5. I control his right wrist with my left hand and rotate with full body weight performing an elbow strike to the side of his face.
6. The elbow strike serves two purposes. It is a strike but also creates a path to slide my right arm under Paul's right arm.

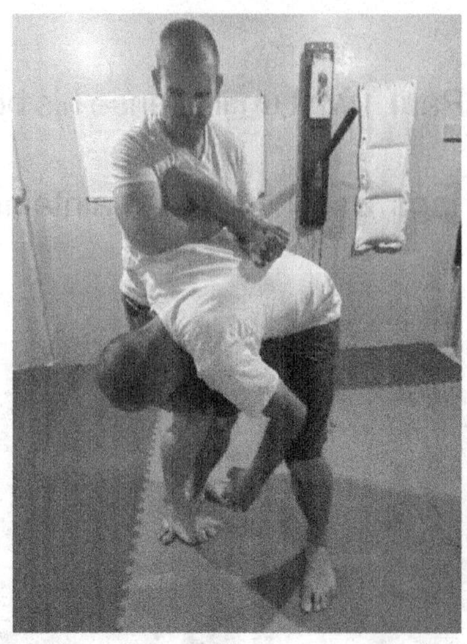

7. I am now positioned to grab my left wrist to set up a figure-four lock.
8. I then rotate to Paul's right side bringing the figure-four lock to his back.
9. With my front foot, I step on his right foot and with my rear foot I trap the back of his right leg to prevent him from turning out of the lock.
10. From this position, you are set up to perform a knee strike.
11. Apply pressure to the lock to damage the arm and shoulder.
12. Push your attacker away to make room to escape.

Bear Hug - Arms Trapped

1. Paul grabs me in a bear hug with my arms trapped.
2. I wrap the inside of Paul's right leg with my right leg to prevent a throw.
3. Anchored to Paul, I wait to sense his body dropping from exhaustion.
4. I then shoot my legs and hips out.

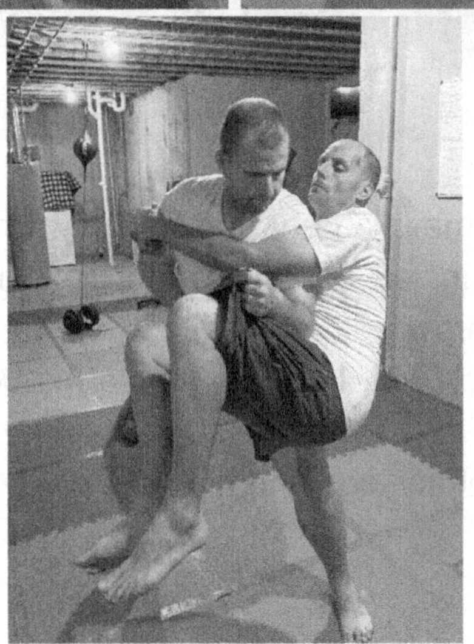

5. I step to my right and perform a strike to the groin.
6. Using a C-step motion, I circle my left leg behind Paul and grab both of his pant legs.
7. Squatting as if I am straddling a horse, I use my thigh as a fulcrum to aid in lifting him.

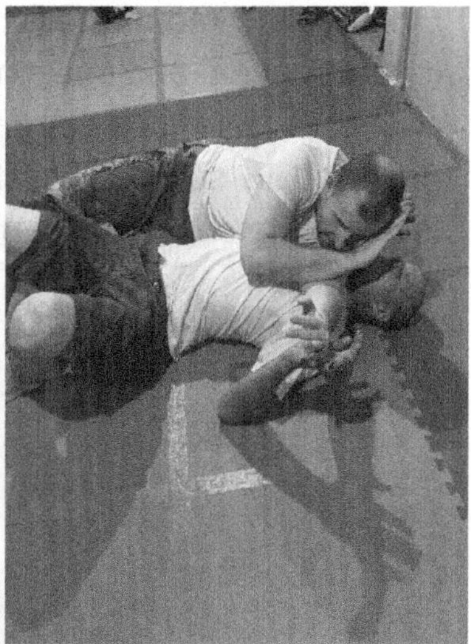
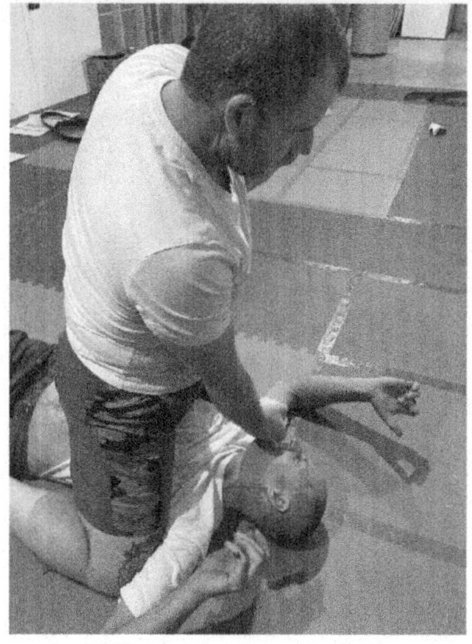

8. As I lift Paul over my thigh, I fall backward with an elbow strike to his sternum.
9. I then cover my face for protection as I make my way over Paul into the mount position. **Note:** I keep low to the ground maintaining a tight connection to his body.

10. Once in the mount position, I strike until the threat is no longer present and make my escape. **Note:** I am not sitting on Paul. My knees are close to his armpits, and I am postured in such a way that my bottom is raised. This lessens the chance of him throwing me off.

Chapter 8 – Punch Attacks

A punch is another common attack. Most people consider a punch to be a closed-hand strike, but for simplicity, I will group all hand strikes into this category. The punch category will include the open-hand strikes and the closed-hand strikes from chapters 4 and 5. Keep in mind that a slap follows the same path as a hook punch, and a shove follows the same path as a straight punch. Therefore, slaps and shoves fall into the punch attack category as well.

What should you expect on the street from a common attacker? The majority of criminals are not trained fighters and do not understand the proper body mechanics to perform a technically correct punch. It is possible to encounter a criminal with some level of training or vast street fighting experience, but most criminals do not spend their time in the gym honing their fighting skills. Just as trained fighters aren't typically on the street looking for someone to mug, trained fighters are in the gym. This does not mean that you should train only for the untrained fighter. You should train as if any attacker you encounter is highly capable of properly throwing any combination of punches, open-hand strikes, or kicks. Training in this manner will give you a significant edge over the general population of untrained fighters.

The number one punch an untrained fighter will deliver is a wide, over-committed hook punch. Not understanding the dynamics required to generate a truly powerful punch, the untrained fighter will pull his or her arm as far back as possible striking you with a large rounding motion using primarily the upper body, shoulder, and arm. Envision the wide, over-committed punches found in the old John Wayne movies. Criminals and street thugs will often attack unsuspecting victims with this type of punch. This is sometimes referred to as a haymaker. A trained fighter will typically use a straight jab, a cross, a tight hook, or an uppercut. A trained fighter will likely lead with a jab or possibly a cross for power.

A punch defense typically has 4 properties.

1. Move
2. Connect
3. Strike
4. Finish

For all punch defense, you should utilize the first property listed above. The move property should reposition you in such a way that you evade the attack and provide yourself with better range, angle, and position to counter. This movement can be performed before or at the same time as the connect property.

The connect property refers to your first contact with your attacker. This will likely be a parry or a block that directly follows your move property. The connect property can also happen simultaneously with your move property. The strike property should follow your connect property.

You now have your move, connect, and strike properties. Taking this concept slightly further, the strike can also be the connect property. Suppose your attacker punches, and you zone to the outside of the attack intercepting his or her punch with a strike. Instead of having the formula:

Punch Defense = Move + Connect + Strike

You now have:

Punch Defense = Move + Strike

In Jeet Kune Do, this concept is called "No Passive Movement". You have eliminated the passive block and went straight for the counter strike.

With proper training and practice, you can also combine the move, connect, and strike into a simultaneous movement. You can move, block, and strike at the same time.

If your strike does not successfully end the altercation, you then move to the finish property. The finish property includes follow-up strikes which utilize the high-low principle along with possible locks and takedowns.

The full formula for a punch defense is as follows, but as shown previously, it is not carved in stone. It is flexible and can be modified as needed.

Punch Defense = Move + Connect + Strike + Finish

The following are commonly encountered punch attacks and defenses.

1. Straight punch (Jab/Cross)
2. Wide hook punch

Straight Punch Defense 1

1. Paul attacks with a straight punch.
2. I guide his fist into my elbow. See the image for reference. This is considered a form of limb destruction and follows the pain principle. This will likely shatter your attacker's hand. You should work this slowly with your partner.
3. I recommend wearing 16-ounce boxing gloves and making light contact.

Straight Punch Defense 2

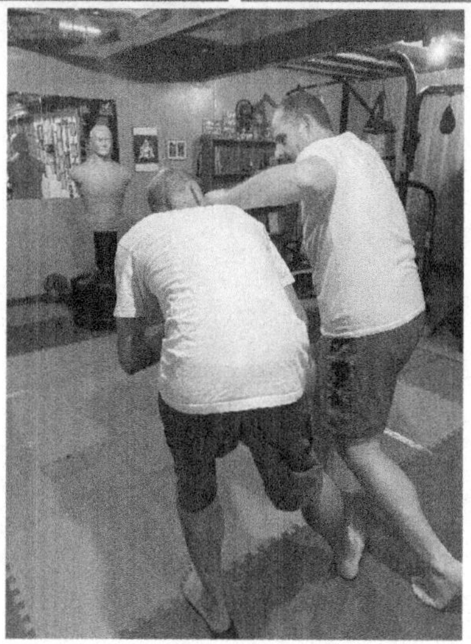

1. Paul attacks with a right jab to my chin.
2. I slip his jab and counter with a right cross to his ribs.
3. I directly follow with a stomp to his knee.

4. After the stomp, I continue my follow-up with a hook to Paul's jawline.
5. You can and should perform additional follow-up strikes to ensure a safe escape.

Wide Hook Punch Defense

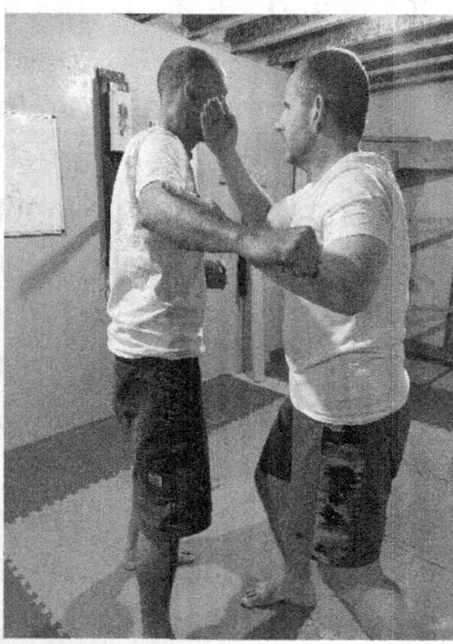

1. Paul attempts a wide hook or haymaker. **Note:** This could also be a slap.
2. I step in, placing my center on his attacking arm performing a two-hand stop. For this block, my left hand sits on top of

my right hand, and I drop my weight into the stop. **Note:** Do not lean forward to drop your weight. Drop your weight downward keeping a good posture.

3. Using what is known as spring energy, my left hand bounces or springs from the stop into a backhand to Paul's jawline turning his head. The backhand serves two primary functions. These two functions support the next technique.
4. Immediately following the backhand, I perform a tight hook to Paul's jawline. The backhand's first function is to provide a guide for the hook. The second function of the backhand is tied to what we know about body reaction. When the head is turned, the natural body reaction is to turn it back to its original position. Now when the hook lands, the force of the hook connects to the jawline along with the force of the head turning back to its original position maximizing impact.

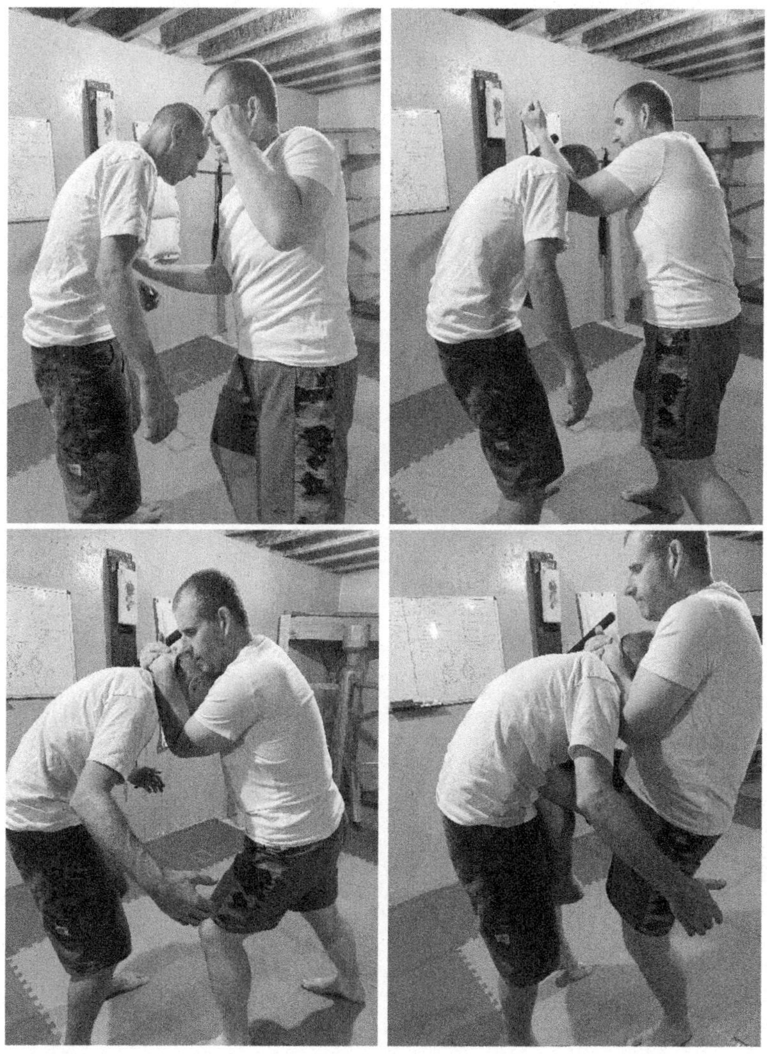

5. After the hook, I perform a right uppercut to Paul's sternum.
6. Following the uppercut, I perform a left brachial stun to the right side of his neck. This is similar to the outside block motion from Karate.
7. From the brachial stun, I immediately clinch the neck and perform a knee strike.

Chapter 9 – Weapon Attacks

In this chapter, I will teach you the theory and application of blunt and bladed weapon defenses. Blunt weapons include items such as sticks and baseball bats. Bladed weapons include items such as knives, machetes, and swords. **Note:** You should always avoid conflict with someone wielding a weapon. If possible, flee the situation.

ALWAYS RUN FIRST IF YOU HAVE THE OPPORTUNITY!

Blunt Weapon Attacks

When dealing with blunt weapons such as a stick or a baseball bat, you can be in one of four locations in relation to the weapon. One, you can be outside the reach of the weapon. Two, you can be within reach of the weapon. Three, you can be beneath the weapon. Four, you can close the distance and be on the inside or the outside of the weapon. If it is a forehand strike, you will close the distance and be on the inside of the weapon. If it is a backhand strike, you will close the distance and be on the outside of the weapon.

If you are outside the reach of the weapon, you will be constantly playing keep up. Your attacker can move forward faster than you retreat and eventually will make contact. If you take more than 2 steps back in a fight without changing your angle and engaging, you are losing.

If you are within reach of the weapon, you will be struck by the weapon. You cannot block a baseball bat or stick in the same way you can an empty-hand attack.

If you can follow the energy of the weapon, you can pass the weapon overhead. Going beneath the weapon in this manner will set you up for a better range, angle, and position to defend yourself. You potentially have a fighting chance. If you successfully pass the weapon, you will need to aggressively attack your assailant, control the weapon, and continue attacking until the threat is no longer present, and then take flight.

The best option is the least natural. When being attacked with a weapon, a person is inclined to step backward. However, closing

the distance by stepping in to meet the attack puts you in a safer position. Let me explain. Most of a stick's power is generated at the last 3 inches of the weapon. As the weapon gets closer to the attacker's hand, the impact of the weapon is lessened. As you step in to close the distance, you begin cutting off the weapon. The location on the weapon that will impact you begins to change. If you step in deep enough, the weapon itself will not hit you. Worst case you would be struck by your attacker's arm. A good rule of thumb is to step in deep enough that you can touch your attacker with your elbow. This should put you within the proper range to not impact with the weapon. Keep in mind, your attacker has another hand that he or she can hit you with. This is called the alive hand. Always be aware of the alive hand when closing the distance. This type of blunt object defense does require some training but is practical. Once you have closed the distance, you will need to control the weapon and strike your attacker continually until he or she is no longer a threat and then take flight.
Below is a list of blunt object attacks and prescribed defenses. As always, violent attacks are dynamic. The attacks and defenses below are only possible scenarios.

1. Baseball bat attack
2. Baseball bat versus baton attack
3. Forehand stick attack

Baseball Bat Attack Defense

1. Paul attempts to strike me above the shoulder with a baseball bat.
2. I close the distance to lessen the impact. As mentioned earlier, the power increases as the impact reaches the last 3 inches of the stick or bat. If possible, the goal is to get in deep enough to take the impact of your attacker's arm rather than the weapon.
3. I catch Paul's arm with the outside of my left arm or elbow. See the images for reference.

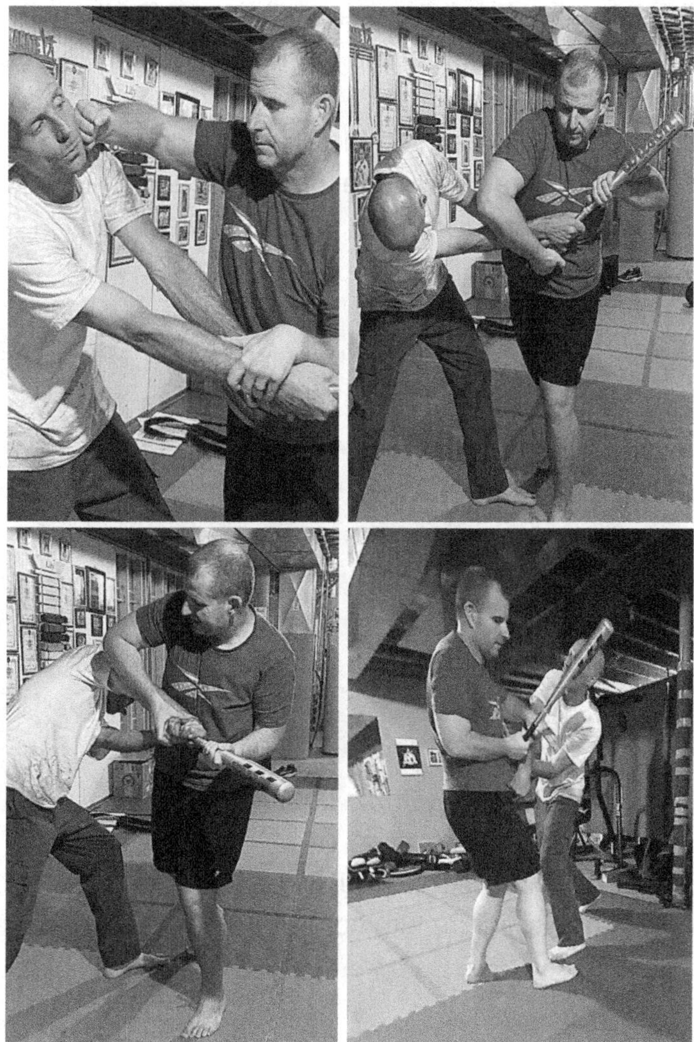

4. With my left hand, I secure Paul's right wrist.
5. I simultaneously execute a right punch to his jawline.
6. The strike immediately wraps around his arms grabbing his left hand on the underside where the tip of the bat handle protrudes. See the image for reference.
7. Using both of my hands, I pull Paul's arms tightly to my body.

8. Then, I slide my left hand down the barrel of the bat. I begin a clockwise rotation of the bat keeping Paul's arms tight to my body.
9. Once the bat reaches the 12 o'clock position, his grip begins to break. By the time it reaches the 1 o'clock position, his grip is broken and he is disarmed.

10. From this point, I strike Paul with a non-life-threatening blow to the knee to injure him so that I can make my escape.

Baseball Bat Versus Batton

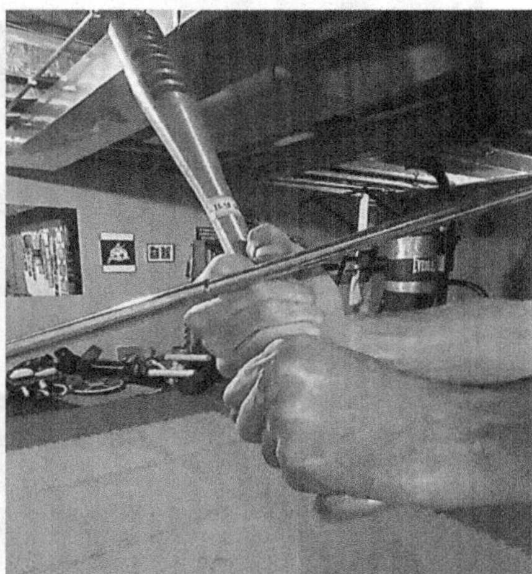

1. In this situation, Paul attempts to strike me with a baseball bat.
2. As Paul swings, I move to position myself out of his range and simultaneously strike his hand(s) with my weapon. In this case, breaking the attacker's hand with your weapon is the simplest disarm. **Note:** Any swing with a blunt or bladed weapon that crosses your centerline will also cross your attacker's centerline. This provides an ideal moment in time to take out your opponent's weapon hand. This does require proper movement and timing on your part.

Forehand Stick Attack Defense

1. Paul performs a forehand stick attack targeting above the shoulder.
2. I zone to Paul's right side and pass his stick hand with my left hand as I perform a hand exchange with my right hand. See the images for reference.

3. Using my left hand, I trap Paul's right arm at the elbow and perform a right elbow strike to his bicep.
4. I immediately perform a right forearm strike to Paul's neck in an attempt to disrupt the blood flow of the carotid artery.

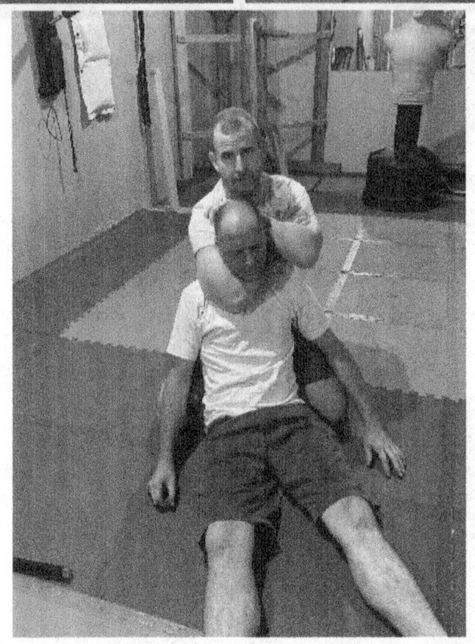

5. I then wrap my left arm under and around Paul's right arm grabbing my right shoulder while applying downward pressure to his neck with a C hand. See the image for reference.
6. From this position, I perform a knee strike to the sternum.
7. Keeping Paul's right arm locked in place, I drop my foot as I simultaneously apply downward pressure to the back of

his neck and rotate my body to the right to perform a shoulder wheel takedown.

8. Once Paul is down, I must maintain a connection with his body to continue to know his position. I do this by initially touching his back with my knee.
9. I now perform a rear naked choke. This choke is not an airway choke but a blood choke. Airway chokes cut off oxygen. Blood chokes cut off the supply of blood to the brain.
10. My right arm slips in closely around Paul's neck. His windpipe should be resting in the bend of my arm. My bicep and forearm should be on each side of his neck to apply pressure to his carotid arteries. See the image for reference.
11. My right arm reaches through grabbing my left bicep.
12. My left hand locks behind Paul's head.
13. I squeeze from the back, and both sides as I slightly raise my body to apply the choke. Unconsciousness will occur in less than 10 seconds. **DO NOT** hold this choke longer than 10 seconds. If you hold the choke too long, your attacker could suffer severe brain damage or death. Done incorrectly with the forearm on the windpipe, it will collapse the airway. Remember escape is our goal. Not killing our assailant. When practicing this with a partner, go slowly. Your goal is to learn the proper positioning of the choke. The throat should be in the bend of your arm. Your forearm and bicep should be on the sides of the neck. Your forearm should never be on the throat. **DO NOT** choke your partner to unconsciousness. Get the position and gently squeeze. As soon as your partner feels the slightest pressure, he or she should tap and you should release.

14. If you are not comfortable performing the rear naked choke, other options are available. Simply striking your opponent is one option. Perform multiple hammer fist strikes to the head. Once you feel your opponent is not a threat, you should immediately escape. **Note:** Do not hit the top of the head! It is the hardest part of the body and will likely hurt your hand more than your attacker.

Bladed Weapon Attacks

Bladed weapons are extremely dangerous. In many ways, at close range, a knife is far more dangerous than a gun. With a gun, you have to get the muzzle pointed away from your body, but knives can move in many directions. It does not take a blade expert to be extremely deadly. If confronted with a bladed weapon, you should always try to escape. If you engage in a knife fight, expect to be injured. Many arts focus on knife fighting. Most of them require fine motor skills which take thousands of repetitions to use successfully or semi-successfully. Even with these fine motor skills, you will still get cut!

When faced with a bladed weapon, you should be aware of vital areas of the body. A good rule of thumb is to protect the arteries on the inside of the legs and arms. The outside of the arms are primarily flesh, muscle, and bone. However, the inside of the arms, starting at the wrists and working the way up to the armpits, contain vital arteries. As the cut moves up the arm toward the armpit, the amount of time required to bleed out decreases. A stab to the armpit severing an artery likely means death.

You should be aware of details surrounding the radial artery, brachial artery, and carotid arteries. The radial artery sits between the radial and ulna bone on the forearm. The brachial artery is on the inside of the arm. This artery is approximately 0.5 inches below the surface. The carotid artery is located approximately 1.5 inches below the surface of the neck. The carotid artery is located on each side of the neck. Severing any of these arteries will result in death in a matter of seconds.

Below is a list of prescribed knife attacks. As mentioned before, acts of violence are dynamic. The attacks below are basic attacks coming from an untrained knife fighter. The motions are large. As the movement compresses into smaller slashes or thrusts, the attacks become much harder to defend. These examples are to provide reference only. To become truly proficient in defending against a knife attack you should seek out a good Filipino Martial Arts school, Kajukenbo school, Krav Maga school, or any self-defense program that has a heavy knife focus.

1. Backhand Knife Attack
2. Stomach Thrust Attack
3. Icepick Attack

Backhand Knife Attack

1. Paul attempts a backhand knife attack.
2. I step to the outside of Paul's attack. **Note:** My position is such that if I miss, I will only take the impact from Paul's arm.
3. I perform a simultaneous stop with my right hand at the wrist and the back side of my left arm slightly above the elbow.
4. This stop wrenches the elbow hoping to break it. This requires the right hand to grab and pull the arm on impact as the left arm pushes. If someone attacks you with a knife, they no longer have the right to ever use that arm again. Break it in as many places as possible.
5. Next, I begin to wrap Paul's arm leading into a figure-four lock.

 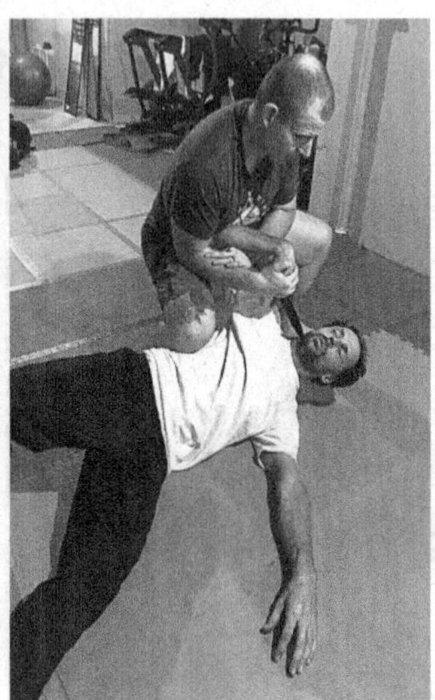

6. The figure-four lock is now complete. **Note:** I have Paul's elbow resting on my bicep to prevent him from pulling his arm out.
7. From this point, using the leverage from the figure-four lock, I take Paul to the ground and apply a gooseneck lock breaking the wrist.

Stomach Thrust Attack

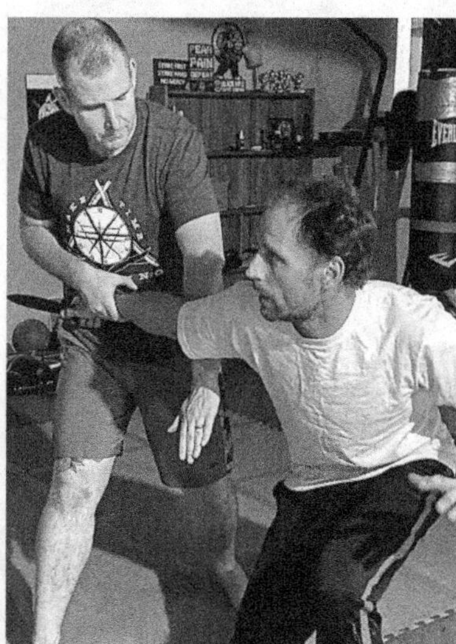

1. Paul thrusts toward my stomach with his knife.
2. I turn to his outside using my left forearm to deflect, and I simultaneously catch and grab with my right hand for control. This is a push/pull wrenching motion to the arm. My left forearm is pushing while my right hand is pulling. The goal is to damage the elbow.

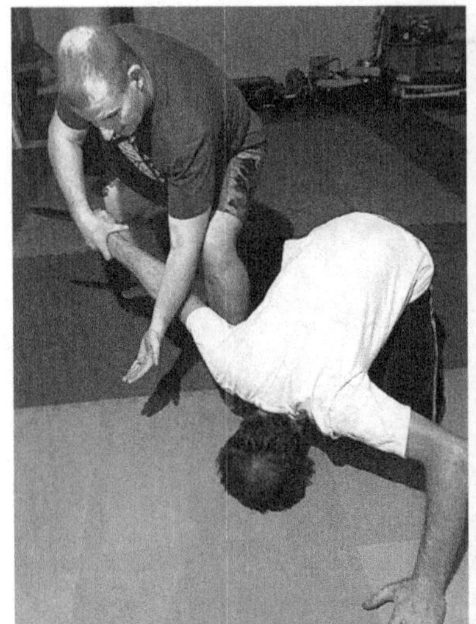
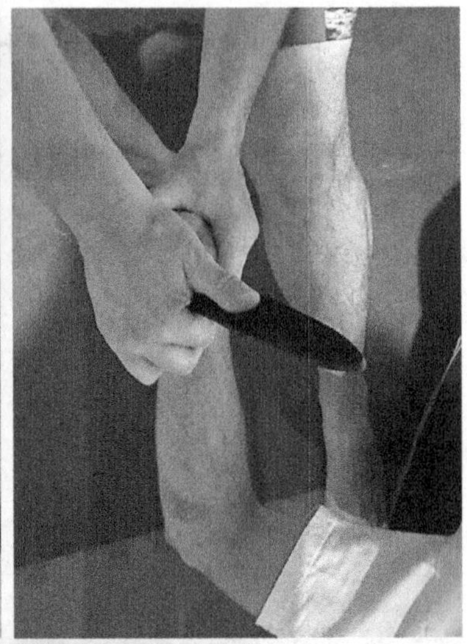

3. I roll my left arm over into an armbar and walk Paul to the ground. See the image for reference. **Note:** This can and should be a break.
4. I then slide my left hand toward his hand and roll his wrist over into a lock. I secure his thumb pad with my left hand and remove the knife with my right hand by pushing against the opening of his fingers. See the image for reference.

5. I continue to control Paul as I back away with the blade pointed in his direction.

Icepick Attack

1. Paul attacks with an icepick attack.
2. I step to Paul's outside passing his attacking hand with my left hand. I guide it down to my right hand for a catch.
3. If Paul strikes with his free hand, he will have no power due to my position on his outside.

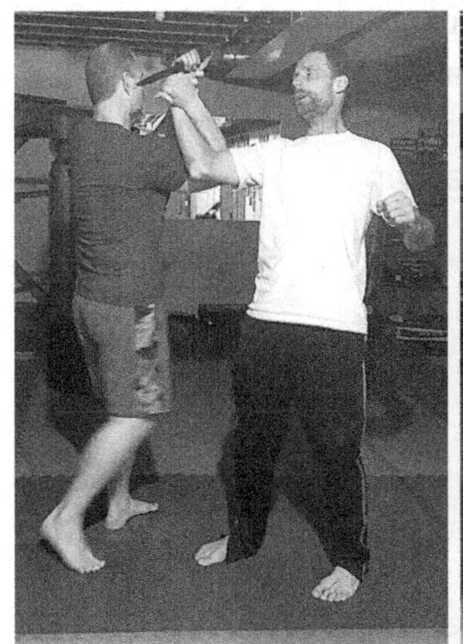
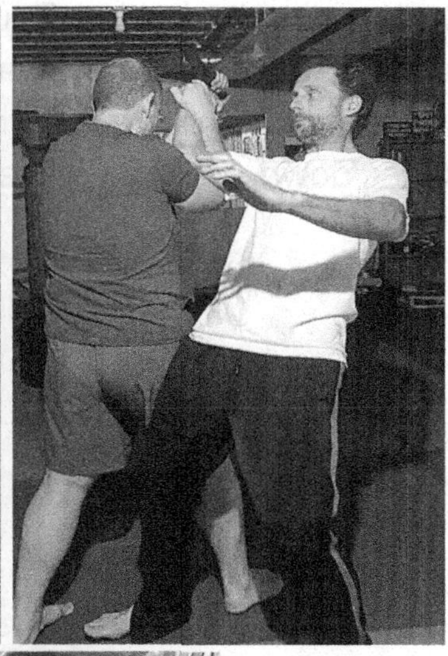

4. Paul attempts to retract his knife hand, and I follow his energy upward.
5. Keeping control with my left hand, I reach around the outside of his arm, grasping the wrist of his knife hand, and perform a variation of a figure-four lock. See the image for reference.

6. I step directly behind Paul with my right leg as I apply downward pressure on the lock. This will break his arm if he resists, but either way, he goes to the ground.
7. Once down, I disarm and escape.

Chapter 10 – Myths of Self-Defense

- **I have a concealed carry permit. I do not need to learn self-defense**.

  Carrying a concealed firearm can be excellent for self-defense. However, you have a limited reactionary time to draw your weapon and be effective. If you miss this window, your firearm could become a detriment to you. You must be able to retain your weapon.

- **A groin kick is the best defense against a man.**

  Since elementary school, men have been protecting the groin region. It is not difficult to deflect a knee or a kick to the groin. A more effective but crude approach is to grab the testicles, squeeze, and forcefully pull. This will cause severe pain and possibly internal bleeding.

- **If you are walking alone, talk to a friend on the phone.**

  You should be alert at all times and focused on your surroundings. Being on the phone gives the appearance of distraction, which screams victim to a criminal.

- **You must be a trained fighter to defend yourself.**

  Although training is beneficial, if you can injure your attacker by any means possible and escape, you have successfully defended yourself. Remember, self-defense is not standing toe-to-toe fighting.

- **Being fit can save your life.**

  Being fit will give you certain advantages such as endurance, speed, and power. Targeting key points of the body during an attack is more important than your fitness level. Focus on the eyes, the nose, the throat, the groin, and the knees. Remember to injure your attacker. Once your attacker is no longer a threat, you should escape. You are not fighting 2-minute rounds for a championship belt. You are fighting for survival.

- **Inflict pain on your attacker.**

  No one enjoys pain. It can make an attacker think twice about his choice to attack. However, many people can fight through the pain. Some people have a naturally high pain tolerance. If your attacker is intoxicated, he or she may not feel pain until the next morning. You must not just inflict pain but injure your opponent so that you can escape without pursuit.

- **Place your keys between your fingers to punch a would-be attacker.**

  Punching requires practice to achieve proper form, power, speed, and accuracy. If you do not practice punching regularly, you will not possess these attributes. If you cannot hit your target with speed and accuracy, you could be wearing brass knuckles and it would not make a difference.

- **You have a black belt; you must know how to defend yourself.**

  Not necessarily! People train in martial arts for many reasons and for some self-defense is not the primary goal. Some people enjoy the tradition of the art. Some like the idea that they are keeping a tradition alive and passing it down to the next generation. Some do it for fitness. Some train as a social activity to make friends. Some people train in martial arts as a fun activity with their children. Some enjoy the sporting and competitive aspects of martial arts. Some train to be technicians perfecting every detail. Some enjoy the reality-based self-defense aspect of martial arts. Why you train plays a role in your ability to defend yourself. If you train with self-defense in mind, you will have a high likelihood of successfully defending yourself.

  What does it mean to be a black belt? It means you have put in a required amount of time in the art. It means you have shown dedication to the art. It means that you are proficient in the curriculum developed by your instructor. In many martial arts, the black belt represents the beginning of learning. Therefore, not all black belts are created equal. Schools focus on different areas. Some focus on traditional art, allowing no variation from the original master's vision. Some schools are progressive and blend arts and remove elements they find no longer beneficial. Other schools focus on sports and competition. Then some focus on self-defense. Your school and curriculum play a role in your ability to defend yourself.

Your personality traits also play a role in your ability to defend yourself. Are you a natural fighter? Some people are born fighters. Others are born more passive. Not everyone has a fighting instinct. If you do not have a fighting spirit, the color of your belt will not save your life. You must have the spirit of a warrior with the mindset that you will not be conquered.

As you can see, many variables come into play when suggesting the color of a belt determines one's ability to defend themselves. Why did this person train and become a black belt? What was his school's focus? What was his focus? Does this person have a warrior spirit?

This leads me back to the Chapter 1 Introduction where I state, "You do not need to be a martial artist to defend yourself.". However, some level of training is important. You should understand the philosophies and principles surrounding self-defense application, and you should have a basic technical skillset. My goal with this book was to provide you with a toolbox containing the essentials. I hope that you walk away after reading with a stronger understanding of self-defense and a feeling of confidence. Keep training and keep it real!